YOU CAN BE SET FREE TOO!

DR. WILLIAM G. BUMPHUS III

Published by Book Writing Pioneer

Cover Design by Book Writing Pioneer

ISBN: Printed in the United States

Table of Contents

CHAPTER ONE

Early Childhood

I grew up in a pretty decent-sized family. I had three sisters and one brother, and my early years were full of excitement and confusion. In those early days, my parents, who were pastors and prison evangelists, would host Christmas programs and giveaways for people in need. We would run around and play all day, having so much fun at those events. I was just a child then and had no real understanding of what was actually going on in our house or the struggles that were happening behind the scenes.

As I got older, I began to notice those struggles more clearly. Our family was always having to move. I like to say it was every six months, but my parents insist it wasn't that often. Still, in many ways, I stayed pretty clueless during those early years, until around fifth grade, when that cluelessness turned into confusion. Kids at school started talking about me and my siblings because of our clothes and our living situations. One time, we were living in the church, and the school bus would pick us up right in front. It was embarrassing. There were some girls on the bus who were just mean and made sure they tried to embarrass us. My little sister always had some fight in her, and one day she must have gotten tired of all the talking because she got off the bus and beat down both of those girls in the alley.

Even though she got that victory and many others, it always felt like we had to argue or fight because of how we lived. What confused me most was that all I ever heard my parents talk about was how good God was. From where I was sitting, God felt absent at best. I started wondering if He was even real based on what I was seeing in the world around me. It seemed like everyone who wasn't following God was living way better than we were. I couldn't ask my parents about it because they were so holy that I knew I'd get some biblical answer that would only confuse me more. By that time, I had already gone to a different school from grades first through sixth, and it didn't seem like this pattern was ever going to end.

As I got older, that confusion slowly turned into rebellion. When I was twelve, my older brother, my best friend, and I went into a convenience store and grabbed a pack of Black & Milds. In my head, I thought there was no way this dude was about to let us young boys walk out of the store with some Blacks, but sure enough, he did. Next thing I knew, we were walking down the street lighting up a Black. My brother and best friend were a little braver than I was. All I could think about was what Mama said, that if I touched anything like that, I was gonna go to hell. So you can imagine how hard my heart was thumping when they passed me the Black.

I tried to be slick and act like I was smoking since it was freezing outside. I figured I'd use the wind as cover, and it worked at first, until the Black went out from lack of smoking. When they realized what I was doing, they lit it again and made me hit it. Oh no, here goes nothing. I took a puff and started coughing so hard my life flashed before my eyes. All I could hear was my mama saying, "I told you; you were gonna go to hell." I looked up, and my brother and best friend were laughing at me. Yeah, this was exactly how I imagined going to hell. Jesus, save me!!!! Anyway, while they were laughing, they started patting my back, and everything settled down. I didn't go to hell. I actually finally felt "cool," and that weekend we walked around the neighborhood smoking the whole pack of Blacks.

I still remember that day clearly. I didn't just feel cool, I felt rebellious. For the first time, I realized that everything my mother told me wasn't necessarily true. I started down a path of rebellion, living a life sort of free from the religion stuff and trying to figure things out my own way. Soon after that, we moved again, this time during my seventh-grade year, and that's when I met K-Man. He was thirteen, dressed fly, and all the girls loved him. He was like the man at school. I hung around him whenever I could and learned what I thought was the art of life from him. His mother would leave him home alone, and we would hang out and break every rule possible. We both liked to sing, so he would call me with two or three chicks on three-way, and we'd do concerts over the phone all night. I didn't become as fly as him that year, but just being around him opened up a whole new experience for me.

For eighth grade, we moved yet again. Different place. Different school. New friends. Even though I stayed in touch with K-Man through those three-way calls, I soon fell in with another group of friends who helped reshape my life even more. I thought K-Man was cool, but this group pushed my desire to rebel to another level. At my school, there were a lot of cliques, not really gang-like, just groups that stuck together. If you weren't part of one, you'd better go somewhere and disappear because someone was going to try you. It wasn't super rough; it was just that kind of environment. This group fit perfectly with what I was on at the time, which was girls. Without boring you with all the details, we hung out heavily that summer, going into my ninth-grade year.

Then one day, everything shifted. They told me we couldn't hang out as much anymore because they had football practice. At that point, hanging out in that big, old, weird-looking white house we lived in wasn't an option, not after all the fun I'd had. So I decided to try out for football. Not really try out, everyone made the team back then. I had no idea what I was doing, but I gave it a shot anyway, just so I could stay close to my crew.

Teenage Years

At this point, we had lived in our house for about two years, and it had started to look like the Jesus that my parents talked about was finally starting to pay off. Things were looking good at school. I wasn't super fly, but I wasn't walking around with old, cheap clothes either. I had developed an understanding on how to live life without getting into major trouble, and I even started to think that knowing God was a cool thing. Life couldn't have been any better, and even though I was horrible in football at the time, I felt like I had almost arrived.

By the end of my freshman year, I had enjoyed being away from home so much with sports that I tried out for every sport in every season. I didn't really know it, but I was actually okay at sports at the time. As a freshman, I made the varsity track team that won state that year, and that took my cool level up a couple of notches. Going into my sophomore year, I decided that I was going to focus on track and basketball, until one day, while walking into the open gym, the football coach made me play football. I remember he shouted, "BUMPHUS, GET IN HERE!" Nothing like feeling wanted. So I went and played wide-out. I wasn't great at it at first, but I was super fast and could run past anybody, so I turned out to be good.

At this point, I was starting to get overwhelmed with all the coolness, and I wanted to be good, so I began to incorporate God in my life. I was a conditional Christian at this point, which meant I only went to God when I needed something. And I figured I only needed Him on Friday before the game. After the game, all bets were off, and I lived as if I didn't even know God. What I will admit is that the whole time I was trying to run away from Him, I always felt His presence. I just chose to ignore Him so that I didn't have to be accountable to Him.

Fast forward a couple of years, I turned out to be really good at football and was blessed to get a scholarship to play at Eastern Illinois University.

College Life

When I got to college, Jesus was the furthest thing from my mind. I mean, I had a relationship with Him and all, but it was definitely only transactional at that point, and those transaction requests were all one-sided. No mama in my business, I could make my own decisions. Shoot, this was what I had always wanted.

I remember my mom would call and ask what I was doing. I'd tell her we were having Bible study. Turns out, they were blunt parties where cats would be so high we'd start philosophizing about the Bible and all kinds of crazy mess. We had the blue light going, music playing, just zoning out. I don't think there was any God in there.

Needless to say, my college life was an up-and-down roller coaster, and being that I was a conditional Christian, I had many times where I needed to beg for the mercy of God to get me out of situations. I remember one time specifically, when I was trying to join This Group, I was doing really bad at making it through the process. One night was so rough that I found myself walking to the football stadium to cry out for help from God. I laid on the high jump mat, stared at the sky, and said that if He was real, He would get me out of this mess that I was in. As soon as I said that, a peace and calm came over me, like everything was going to be okay. The next day, that process ended, and I made it through such an arduous task.

That experience would prove to be vital in my search for the realness of God. But even after that, I still had my doubts. Those doubts would soon be clarified when I had my encounter with the woman who led me to Christ.

The Day I got "Saved"

I wasn't the greatest athlete, but I had clearly made a name for myself on campus. I was the president of my fraternity at the time, and that alone brought about a sense of responsibility, which for me also turned into a little bit of arrogance. I thought I was God's gift to everyone, and women were not exempt.

One day, while walking in the yard, I saw this young lady who I thought would be my next project. I checked my hair (I was bald then too), made sure my teeth didn't have any food in them, and I went in for the kill. As I approached her, I started to feel this nervousness come all over me. Though I didn't realize it at the time, I would later understand that this feeling was God's Spirit trying to get my attention.

When I got about five feet away, she turned around and stopped me in my tracks. Before I could get a word out, she said, "God has been talking to me about you, and He told me you need to get your life together before you mess it up." Then she said, "You need to get saved."

Every fiber in my being just got weak, and I stood there bawling and crying on her shoulders. Needless to say, that day, in that moment, I accepted Jesus Christ as my personal Lord and Savior. I will always remember the peace of God that came over my life right then. The day I got "saved" was so enlightening to me, and I was so excited to see what God had in store for my future.

I would like to end the story here and say that from that point on, I lived a life dedicated to God and never looked back, but that certainly was not the case. It would be many years and many trials before I get to that place. For now, I will say that this moment set my life on a course, one that would, along the way, bring me to a point where I resented God even more for many years.

CHAPTER TWO

Gung Ho for Jesus

Once I had given my life to Christ, I went gung-ho into my purpose of sharing the gospel. I stopped drinking, smoking, and hanging out as much with the frat. I spent my time telling people about Jesus and how great He was. Of course, on a college campus, you're going to deal with a lot of people who don't believe, and I remember going back and forth with people about the Bible, pleading my case based on the limited knowledge I had. I led one of my good friends and roommates to Christ, and I felt like I was God's new gift to the ministry.

At this point, I was also starting to see what I thought were the fruits of my labor for Christ. I played football with some really, really talented guys. One of them was my quarterback, who went on to be an NFL legend. I always believed that mine and God's plan was for me to go to the NFL, and with all the attention of the other great players I played with, it looked like I was about to get my shot and God was about to come through.

I came into camp that year feeling the best I had ever felt. This new life with Jesus was just so sweet, and I was ready to go on the ride. I had started getting more attention from people. My coaches were satisfied with me. I felt like I was on top of the world, and it was all due to Jesus and His great plan for my life. But I also started getting a little too arrogant. I began to talk as if it was all me and my ability, even though I knew it was God.

At that time, I was super close to the lady who had led me to Christ. She would tell me to stop having the big head or God was going to take my legs. I would laugh and say things like, "Yeah right. God wouldn't do anything like that to me. I'm too valuable to Him." It was all a joke, and we never really thought too much about it.

Our football team went into the first couple of games on fire. I think I had about five catches and four TDs, and it seemed like things were about to take off. We went into our next game, which was a big one, and everyone was talking about it. I remember calling my father and going through our ritual of speaking life over me and talking about good outcomes. He would always pray over me and tell me to call him after the game. Off I went to be great again, still in awe of what God was doing in my life.

The Thing I Have Greatly Feared

I remember going out to the field, and it was a weird day. There were so many people there, it seemed, and everything around me on the field felt super close. It felt like I was in a zone, and I remember thinking, *This must be what God's supernatural presence feels like.* I'm telling you, I felt something that day, and it seemed like it was a good thing.

As the game went along, my coach called a special reverse play for me. Remember earlier when I said I felt God's Spirit on me before I got saved? I had that very same feeling when this play was called. It seemed like everything just slowed down around me, like I was the only one there. The quarterback snapped the ball, I came around on the reverse, no one was there. I got about twelve yards up the field, and right when I was about to step out of bounds, the safety from the other team hit me low. I went out of bounds, and it felt like my leg was just hanging.

They called for the trainers, and I remember just going blank. I didn't black out or anything. I think I went into a spiritual shock because I felt no pain and heard no voices. It was just blank, that's the best way I can describe it.

They took me in the locker room, let me sit on the floor, gave me the bad news, and walked out. There I was, finally alone with God in the same spot where I had just received prayer and words of encouragement from my father. I finally spoke, and it wasn't good at all. It was like every word that I hadn't said over the last few months because I was "saved" came pouring out in that moment. I think I called God everything I could think of because I just couldn't understand how He could let this happen to me after I had been so faithful to Him.

I was finally at a point where I believed everything about God, and here I was, done for the season with a torn ACL and MCL. As I sat there devastated and crying, I remember God speaking to me at that moment and saying, "If you live for Me, I'll make your life better than you could ever dream or imagine." I wiped my tears off my face, got dressed, and went out to watch the rest of the game.

Of course, after an injury like that, everyone tries to help by offering sympathy, thoughts, and prayers. But to me, it only made it worse. I remember going to church the next day, and when the lady who led me to Christ, the same one I had joked with about God taking my legs, saw me on crutches during the service, she screamed with so much agony and pain and ran out of the room. I can still hear the pain in her voice. She thought that her words might have played a part in my injury.

Of course, we knew it was the enemy, but nonetheless, it was still a hard blow for both of us to take at the time. We spent so much time praying over my body and over my life that this injury became a major shaking in my faith.

The First Official Backslide

After hearing from God in that locker room, I figured God and I were still on the same track of me playing professional football. I remembered my father, over all the years, talking about faith, and was in full faith that God would supernaturally heal me and my knee. I just knew that I would come back stronger, faster, and better, and I knew that God was going to use my story as one of redemption and triumph.

Though I did come back earlier than expected, it wasn't the same for me, and I began to get discouraged. I slowly started falling back into my old life and patterns, and I developed a secret resentment toward God because of what I felt He had done to me. Since I had spent the last year or so preaching to everyone, I did my best to keep up the Christian walk, but my deep anger toward God at that time prevented me from fully walking it out any longer. One of my lowest points during that season was watching the roommate I had led to Christ backslide because of me.

During my decline of falling away from God, we were at the frat house playing dominoes one day. One of my buddies, who I had been secretly smoking weed with, passed me the blunt in front of my saved roommate. I couldn't act like I didn't indulge, so I grabbed the blunt and puffed away. My roommate asked me what I was doing, and I told him that it was alright, God didn't really care anyway. He put his bones down and hit that blunt so fast, like he had been wanting to do that for years.

In my heart, I felt bad that day. I knew what had just happened and the effect it would have on him. I was at a low point, and I couldn't even go to God about it because I blamed Him for being there.

I went on to finish my football career at Eastern. I did come back and play that year and gave a valiant effort to make it to the next level, but it didn't turn into anything. I played some Arena II football for a few games, but my new drinking and partying habits messed that up. I had graduated as well, and there was nowhere to go but back home to try and figure out life.

Up until that point, I didn't really have a plan other than playing football. With that all but gone, I loaded up the Cady, and just like that, that stage of my life was over. I had met my wife (girlfriend at the time) in college, so I blindly moved us back to Indy and began the next phase of my life. Boy, was it an adventure, one that would eventually take me down a path where my resentment toward God would come full circle.

CHAPTER THREE

Home Again

When I first came back home, in the back of my mind, I still believed the plan for me was to play football. I started trying out for more arena teams, but all were to no avail. I wrestled with God because I felt like He wasn't helping. Heck, I wasn't even seeing any light in the tunnel.

I started going to my parents' church and became active in the ministry. Soon after, I was ordained as a minister and began going into prisons and conducting services like my parents. By then, God had been really good to them, and I began to see the fruit of all those years of them both doing the work of ministry. It seemed like my parents were proud of me, and I felt "The Call" of God on my life, but at that time, I wasn't really wanting to go that route.

For one, I still had a secret resentment towards God for how He let Satan mess up my football career and didn't do anything about it. In many ways, I was still waiting on the promise made to me in the locker room and was doing my best to wait on that. Secondly, at the time we were "STRUGGLIN." We lived with my sister for a while in a spare bedroom and slept on a roll-out couch. It was so old we could feel the springs coming through the mattress. At the same time, my wife got pregnant, and that spring bed was not going to work.

We ended up moving into an apartment, but with me still pursuing football and her having the baby, we eventually got so far behind in the bills that we were evicted.

With all of this happening, and things not going well at all in Indianapolis, we decided to move to St. Louis to be closer to her family and friends. I was still pursuing football, so I wasn't excited about getting a job at the time. I was still standing on my faith and believing God was going to do something amazing. Of course, that's fine when you're chasing a dream on your own, but with a wife and a one-year-old daughter, that dream has a small window.

After a while, that dream began to become an issue, not only for my wife, but for others as well. I understood how they felt, but they didn't have a "plan" with God, so I largely ignored everyone. That only brought about more secret resentment and anger towards everyone. The whole time we were in another state, I kept feeling this draw to go back home and do more ministry. I didn't like that feeling at all because I remembered what we went through as kids and how my parents' life wasn't the best in the beginning.

I remember telling God flat out, "I am not doing prison ministry if I have to go through the same struggle my parents went through." I still had a strong desire to play football, and ministry would get in the way of that. So I ignored that feeling for a while, until things got so bad for me in St. Louis that I finally decided we were coming back to Indy.

When I made the decision to come back, I made what I thought was a deal with God. I told Him I would come back and give football another try for a couple of more months, and if I wasn't playing by then, I would give up that dream and work in the ministry. They say if you want to make God laugh, tell Him your plans. I think that may have been true in this case. Because things just got funnier from there.

Cut Game

When we got back to Indy, we had to move in with my other sister. By then, we were definitely on the path of my parents, and I didn't like it one bit. I felt like I knew what God wanted me to do, but again, I wasn't going to do it this way. God would just have to use someone else because I didn't want it like this.

Then one day, finally, after all the trying and making decrees, I got another chance to play football. I was invited to a camp in Appleton, Wisconsin, for an arena team. I promise, this was all a God thing. I remember driving down on the last little bit of money we had, and I was looking for some gloves for the tryout. I prayed and asked God to come through, and sure enough, in a place we would have least expected it, some football gloves were just sitting there randomly. I knew God was with me.

I got to the tryout, and the coach had heard of me to the point that I didn't even have to work out. He started using me to demonstrate the drills. I left there, invited to camp without even trying out. Clearly, my plan with God was in full effect, and I just knew He was about to do what we had always talked about. I was finally about to become a star.

I went to camp fully persuaded that this was part of the plan. Things were going really well. I had developed a reputation for being a man of God. The quarterback was a strong Christian, and a few of us formed our own little group of believers on the team. We had Bible study and prayed together every night.

Camp was going well, and as we approached the first cut game, things looked good for me making the team. With my wife and daughter being back in Indy, I started to miss them, but I figured that would just be part of the story God would use in the end. I remember watching the movie *Rocky,* the one where he says, "Yo Adrien, we did it." I would tell myself that this was going to be my story, and I even sent clips to my wife saying this would be our moment. Man! This was it, I just knew God was fulfilling His promise to me, and I was ready for the ride.

The "cut game" happened to fall on Easter Sunday that year. Because my teammates saw me as the preacher, we decided to have an Easter chapel service before the game, and they voted for me to preach. I don't remember what I preached on, but at the end, when I gave the altar call, almost everyone in the room raised their hand and gave their life to Christ. I remember thinking, *Wow*! Even the head coach raised his hand and got saved. I felt so good about that and was so hyped for the game.

But once the game started and I got in, it was like I had no desire to be there anymore. I remember the ball came my way, and I didn't even raise my hands to try to catch it. I was so confused. I had waited for this opportunity for so long. God had worked so many miracles to get me there. Why was I feeling like this?

We drove back home that night on the bus and watched a film on the ride. I was disgusted with my performance. Of course, I questioned God and sat there in shock, feeling like the opportunity had slipped through my fingers.

When we got back to Appleton, I remember looking at the TV, and whatever I was watching made a statement: "Sometimes we have to give up our dreams so others can have *theirs.*" At that moment, I felt my heart melt because I knew the football dream was over for me. That season had ended, and I knew God was calling me into ministry.

The next day was cut day. It was also going to be a break, and my wife and daughter were coming to visit. When I had that realization the night before, I called my wife and told her to come early because I knew that I would be going home. The next morning, some of my teammates told me I would be fine and would at least make it to the second cut, but I was convinced the feeling had left, and I was going home either way.

I went into my meeting with the coaches, and I remember the room feeling super dark. The first thing the coach said was that he appreciated my sermon the day before. He said that it was the best sermon he had ever heard and thanked me for it.

Then he cut me... LOL!!!

CHAPTER FOUR

Back Home Again, Again!

As you can imagine, that ride back to Indy from Wisconsin was a rough one. Even though I had made my deal with God, almost immediately, my anger and resentment toward Him swelled up again. I felt so disappointed, yet I had to walk around like everything was good and my faith was still strong.

When I came back to church, everyone seemed excited about me being home. I remember feeling like they were lame because I thought they didn't believe in me for some reason. Come to find out, my mother had been telling them how she had been praying that I would come back home. Of course, that only added to my frustration with God. Even worse, in the middle of all of that, we were still living with my sister.

That situation became a strain on everyone involved. I was working three jobs at the time, trying to get us out of that house. It was a small three-bedroom place. My sister had three kids and a live-in boyfriend, so things were definitely getting out of hand. After a few months, we were finally able to move out again into our next home. It was a two-bedroom shotgun double in the middle of the hood.

Things were fine until it got cold outside and we started hearing little noises in the front room at night. At first, I thought someone was trying to break in. After a few days, I realized the intruders were mice. That definitely didn't sit well with my wife, so I began trying every method possible to get rid of them.

We started with sticky traps. The problem was that when the mice got stuck, you could hear them all night trying to break free. At one point, I think I was killing four or five a night. Then I switched to the traps coming up from the basement, but all night long, all you would hear was "SNAP." Eventually, we got them under control, but it was a struggle.

The Falling Away

By then, I was fuming at God, and I could feel myself steadily drifting away from Him. I stopped praying and reading the Bible as much. I pretty much only opened it when preparing for services. Other than that, I was too angry with God to do much else. In my heart, I really wanted to follow Him, but I just couldn't get past the hurt from football and now this life I felt stuck in. Everything I had asked God for regarding His plan for my life had failed, and the thoughts of walking away from Him grew stronger and stronger.

At that time, I was working as a substitute teacher during the day, coaching football in the evening, and working third shift at a warehouse. I was so angry with God that I started to pull back from ministry. I began to dislike going into prisons because I felt like they didn't want to hear from someone who hadn't been where they had been. I would share my testimony about football and college, but I felt like I had nothing to show for it since I hadn't made it. I did everything I could to make my story sound interesting, but the looks on their faces told me they weren't really moved by what I had to say.

We moved out of the house with the mice and into another double, but this one was in a nicer area. I remember praying and asking God to show me a sign that He was still there. The very next day, we went to check out the house, and in the basement was a pool table. I took that as a sign from God because He knew how much I had always wanted a pool table in my house. We applied for the place and, miraculously, got it.

Even though I knew God was still working with me, it wasn't enough to take away the anger I still felt toward Him.

We moved into the house, and I started thinking about what I was gonna do with the rest of my life. I knew I wouldn't be taking over the ministry anytime soon because both of my parents were still very active, so I was limited in what I was doing there. At the warehouse, I started getting noticed for my hard work. Within six months, I was promoted to supervisor, but it still wasn't enough money to keep up with the bills.

That began to cause trouble in the marriage, on top of me being gone all the time and still being behind on bills. I also had a problem with trying to force my wife to trust God and live by this concept of faith. The sad thing about it was that I was trying to force her to live and understand something that I wasn't fully committed to myself.

These problems persisted for a while, and it all came to a head one day when I came home from one of my jobs and my wife was moving her stuff out of the house. Man! Another blow. This life that God had given me was definitely turning out the wrong way, and at that point, this whole plan of God wasn't working. I felt like I was holding up my end of the deal, but He wasn't, and to me, that wasn't cool.

Devastated by all of it, I went through a series of emotions that marked the beginning of the downward spiral my life started to take that day.

If you've ever been in a situation where your significant other leaves you, you know that in the next few days, you go through different phases of emotion. I think mine started with anger, and that rage turned into a very messy house. Everything she left ended up somewhere else in that house. When I ran out of things to break, I would pick them up and try to break them all over again.

I felt so alone. I felt like I had done everything God asked me to do and everything she had asked of me. I felt like she wasn't real because she couldn't stick by me during tough times. I felt like God was absent and wanted nothing to do with me. I went through those few days without telling or talking to anyone. I was angry and tried to pray, but to me it all felt pointless.

On the fourth day, I woke up and said I was going to start rebuilding my life on my own—without God, without my wife—by myself.

Over the past few years, I hadn't drunk any liquor. I had been holding out, waiting on God, and felt like drinking would mess up whatever blessing He had coming my way. But on that day, I decided to make an exception. My plan was to go get some cleaning supplies and a wine cooler.

Now, where I come from, a grown man better not get drunk off a wine cooler. I knew I was gonna be fine, so I grabbed a six-pack of Seagram's Bahama Breeze wine coolers. I got home, put on some music, and started cleaning while drinking the Bahama Breeze. By the time I made it to the basement, I was using the broom as a microphone, singing love songs and practicing old-school Alpha strolls. I had gone through the whole pack of coolers and was drunk as a skunk.

The next day, I felt terrible about getting drunk. At the same time, that drink had been refreshing. It helped take the edge off the anger and heartbreak, even though the pain was still there.

Without going into all the details, after about three months of working on things, I was blessed to reconcile with my wife. I moved out of the old house where I was behind on rent and into an apartment with her. By then, I was really making a name for myself at the warehouse. Upper management started showing interest in me, and because of my education, I qualified to be fast-tracked into management.

After a year or so, I was promoted to a management position and was bringing in a pretty decent amount of money. Just when we thought we were finally getting over the hump financially with both of our incomes, we soon started struggling again.

Remember earlier when I said that one night of drinking started the downward spiral in my life? Well, during that three-month period, along with a new drinking and clubbing habit, I also developed a bad gambling addiction. Almost every payday, I would get off work at 6 a.m. and drive straight to the casino. Since my wife was at work, I was able to hide it for a while—until I started spending bill money trying to win my money back.

It was rough. In an effort to get me back on track, my wife told my parents about my new habits, hoping they could talk some sense into me. Of course, they couldn't change me. I think I lied to them and told them she was overreacting, but I'm sure they could tell something was off because I hadn't been going to church as much and blamed it on my new job.

Truthfully, on the inside, I was so mad at God and my wife by that point that I really didn't care what my parents thought. In the back of my mind, I was also mad at my mother for praying that I would come home from football. As you can imagine, I had a lot of built-up anger inside. I couldn't talk to anyone—including God—because I felt like they were all complicit in the mess going on in my life.

Since God hadn't done what I thought He should have done by then, I slowly drifted further away from church. I also picked up another habit—clubbing. I was so angry with life that I decided I was going to do everything my way and just wait for God to come get me whenever He was ready to do something with me. I guess I told myself I was making up for everything I had missed trying to follow God in those earlier years.

Partying became the thing for me. I was used to it from college, and to me this just felt like college life all over again. I was living it up, hanging out with my crew. Even though I was still angry inside, going out and drinking seemed to help me cope.

All of that changed one night while I was out with my crew. That night would go on to be the night that would set my life on another path—one that would lead to the ultimate destruction of me.

CHAPTER FIVE

VIP

On one of those nights of partying, we linked up with a good friend of mine and his crew. Up until that point, in all my years of clubbing, I had never been in the VIP section. Growing up and going to clubs, nobody ever told me about the section that keeps you away from the normal crowd and gives you the chance to enjoy the scene with the high rollers.

That night, I was introduced to that life.

I would ask for a drink, worried about the price, and the waiter would say, "No, everything in this section is free." Man, I was living. I enjoyed every minute of it. Because this crew was rumored to be dealing drugs, I didn't want to get too close, but I did what I could to fit in and enjoy the night.

At the end of the night—and this was the part that impacted me—when it was time to pay the bill, I watched these dudes start pulling out stacks of cash. Hundreds on top of hundreds, with plenty more to spare. I thought, *Man, I'm struggling to pay bills, and these dudes are out here just blowing money.*

That was it.

I made up my mind that I was done with struggling. I was going to figure out a way to live like that every day. So I set out a plan to make it happen.

Make Money, Money!

After a couple of weeks of trying to figure out how I was going to make that kind of money, I was stuck in my thoughts. The only idea that kept coming to mind was selling drugs, but I knew the ultimate outcome of that, so I didn't want any part of it.

Frustrated, one day while sitting at work, I had this thought: *How can I get some of this stuff out of this facility without anyone knowing?* Security was tight, so taking it out the front door wasn't an option. For a while, every night, I tried different methods of getting the items out, and none of them worked.

Finally, one day I had a bright idea. What if I didn't take it out the front door at all, but instead had the package delivered to my front door? Our company had just changed the way we handled labels, and I remembered that we could change the address if we had the information.

One day, when no one was looking, I grabbed a laptop coming down the line. I acted like the label was messed up and attempted to print another one—except this time, I put my address on it. Not knowing whether the plan would work, I placed the new label on it and sent it on its way.

I worked the rest of my shift thinking, *Man, that was stupid. That package is not going to show up at my house. What was I thinking?* I finished work, forgot all about it, and went home.

That One Package

I was working third shift at the time, so I came home and went to sleep—probably dreaming about making more money. When I woke up later, I wasn't even thinking about that package anymore. I had already assumed it wasn't coming.

I went downstairs and started my normal routine, waiting for my wife to get home. Around 5 p.m., she walked in with a package in her hand.

My eyes lit up when she said, "Did you know you had a package out front?"

I grabbed it in disbelief and opened it excitedly. Sure enough, it was the same laptop I had shipped to myself. In that moment, I felt like I had cracked the code.

I didn't even realize what type of laptop it was. I figured it was just a basic model, but it turned out to be one of the best on the market at the time. It had a swivel monitor and was one of the first touchscreen models. It was Bluetooth compatible, which was rare back then.

I looked it over and searched online to check the price. It was a $1,200 laptop.

My wife immediately assumed it was stolen because there was no way we could afford something like that. She told me to get it out of the house right away, so I found someone to sell it to. Since it was Christmas time, I advertised it as the perfect Christmas gift. Within hours, it sold for $500—and just like that, I was in a new business.

With the money, I bought my daughter a doll for Christmas and got myself a 32-inch TV and a PlayStation.

For the next couple of weeks, I sat at work waiting for the fallout from a missing package. To my surprise, there was no mention of it. About a week later, anxious to see if the plan would work again, I did it again. This time, I grabbed a couple of laptops and a flat-screen TV.

Since it was clear my wife wasn't going to be part of this, I had the items shipped to another house. Sure enough, they arrived there too, and I sold them within days.

No one at work mentioned anything. No one checked on the missing items. At that point, I was on a roll. Twice a week, I would get a package, and things were going really well. But I knew I had to find a way to make more money. I was only grabbing two or three items at a time, and with this new lifestyle I was living, I needed money faster.

That problem would be solved sooner than I thought.

AHHH!

Probably twice a week, we used to get these big shipments in from China. I didn't know what they were. I just saw that the boxes were always plain-looking with a "Made in China" stamp. I never really thought much about them, but with my new business venture, I figured I might as well find out what was inside, in case it was something I could sell.

So one day, I grabbed one of these boxes and opened it up. I tell people, when I opened that box, I saw a light from heaven and heard a sound like, "AHHH." I say that because when I opened it, I saw rows and rows of Apple iPhones. There were three boxes, with 10 phones each in the boxes. This was the lick I had been waiting for. I just took the whole box. With these, I no longer needed to take a bunch of other stuff. This one box was enough.

To put it into better perspective, these were the first-generation iPhones, which means they were in high demand and hard to access. I had a whole box of them. They were going in the store at the time for about $600, but I was selling them for $300 a pop. Needless to say, that box was gone in a day, and the demand for more rose drastically.

This system of one box lasted for about three weeks. The demand and money were so high that I had to figure out a way to get more out at a time. That number started going up to three or four boxes for a while. The main reason for this was that I was trying to get a gauge on what security was seeing and if the devices were being tracked. They didn't seem to be, so I ramped up the operation.

Soon, I wasn't just getting phones—I was getting tablets, computers, and everything else Apple made at the time. I was easily bringing in $15,000–$20,000 a week at this point, and I was not in the business of slowing down.

Of course, with all the money I was making, I was spending it as soon as I got it. Taking trips, partying, and buying just about anything. I was a whole nut with this thing.

The funny thing is, during all of this time, just like in the past, God was around, dealing with me in my head. I was having fun, but it all came at a spiritual cost. On the inside, I was in turmoil—mainly because I knew what was going to happen when I got caught (because everybody gets caught). And secondly, because I knew I was breaking the Father's heart. But I was so mad at Him at the time, I felt like I was paying Him back for all the letdown I had suffered on His behalf. (That was just my reasoning.)

Making My Own Bed

Between the operation, money, and partying, I was able to deal with all the spiritual warfare stuff. I was completely out of the church at this point and had no plans of going back any time soon. I truly believed that I wasn't going to play with God. I wasn't going to be in church and, at the same time, be living foul on the outside, so I continued to make excuses for not going to church. My main excuse was that I was out of town every weekend.

On one of these out-of-town trips, I was talking to one of my homeboys from college. I was telling him about my operation, and he was like, "Dude, put me on." Of course, I had to do that, so he gave me an address, and I started sending stuff his way. This proved to be super lucrative for me. I would leave my house with about $2,000, go to his state, pick up money (usually about $40K every other week), we'd party off some of that money for the weekend, then do it all over again. This was my life now. I had gotten so deep into it that stopping at this point was just not an option—not because I didn't want to, but because I was so wrapped up in the image and the life that it just had a stronghold on me.

By now, I had a team of people working the operation with me. The funny thing is, most of them had no idea they were involved in anything illegal. I had a team of cats who I would party with knew what was going on, but it was a tight-knit circle. I had moved into a bigger house by now, and figured it was time to slow down. Again, I knew this needed to happen, but I didn't know how it would.

At this point, God had been dealing with me so much that He literally started warning me to stop. I received three distinct warnings that I knew were from God. The first came from one of my good work buddies. He wasn't involved in what I was doing, but he eventually put two and two together. One day, while we were on our way to the casino, he told me that God had come to him in a dream or something. I don't remember all the details, but I just remember him saying that it was time to stop. I figured it was from God because this guy wasn't really a "God" dude—we'd never had any real conversations about God. So, him mentioning that was a giveaway that it was from God.

After that conversation, I stopped for a few weeks. Because I didn't stop partying and spending money, I started to see the money go down, and the urge kicked back in. I remember feeling so bad that I started up again. I would pray before I did it, "God, bless me in my stupidity." That was my prayer (how stupid is that?). I would continue for a few more weeks before I got my second warning.

One night while working, I got a call from my boss to come to his office. When I first got the call, I really thought the gig was up and he was calling me to his office to take me down. When I got there, he told me I was suspended because one of my employees had said I did something against policy and procedure, and I was being suspended pending investigation. I was suspended for a week.

Of course, I went back to my usual mold of praying for God to fix it. It turned out to be nothing, but again, I knew it was God giving me yet another warning.

That week I got back to work, I made the decision that I was going to do one last big score and be done—that was my promise to God, and I was going to keep it. Little did I know, I wouldn't really have a choice.

Psalm 139:8b says, "If I make my bed in hell, behold, you are there," signifying that God will walk with you and knock on your door even until you take your last breath. But if you make your bed there, it's your fault, and you have to deal with that decision. I mention that because I always think about that scripture when I remember the third and final warning God gave me. I won't go into all the details that this warning came with, but I will say that God literally warned me with every move I made that day. And I was so far gone that I just simply overlooked all of them, even though they were clear as day.

One Last Time

When I arrived at work that night, I had a whole plan for what was about to happen. Because I knew it was going to be my last hit, I planned to get as much as I could this one last time. I had all my addresses set, and I was good to go. One last huge score. Things were going as normal, when all of a sudden, about 600 yards away, I saw security parked in the cut. They were so far down that I normally wouldn't even look down there, but something made my head look up and focus on them.

I instantly thought I should postpone for the night, but this score was so big, and I had so many people waiting for the shipment, that I simply ignored the car, thinking they were just down there chilling. I went about the normal operation—got all the stuff boxed up, made my labels, counted it, loaded it, and sent it out.

As soon as I sent it out, that feeling I got when I blew my knee out in college immediately came over me as that truck rolled out of the building. As I'm watching the truck turn, I also see that same security car roll right behind them. Oh shoot! Can you imagine what went through my head when I saw that? I didn't know whether to run or what to do. I immediately grabbed my phone to call the driver and tell him to come back, but ironically, my phone wouldn't go through. Panicking, I kept trying to call, to no avail. Then, all of a sudden, he answers and says, "Hey boss, security pulled me over and they want you to come down here."

Dude! This was it! They caught me. As I was walking up, I saw them high-fiving and hugging each other. It was like a huge celebration, and rightfully so. I had been getting them for a while, and I'm sure it had been giving all of them fits.

They put me in the back of the security car, and off I went to the security office. On the way there, my mother's voice popped into my head again, this time saying, "Any time you get in trouble, you need to call on the name of Jesus." This definitely qualified as one of those times, so in the back of that car, I asked God for any help He could give me at that moment. Without fail, I heard His voice, and it said, "TELL THE TRUTH."

I immediately said, "I rebuke you, devil." I just knew this was not God telling me to do that.

Sure enough, they got me in that room, showed me all kinds of stuff. I mean, they had done their homework. They showed pictures of everyone involved, addresses, a transcript of the phone call they tapped—everything.

So, I confessed and put all the blame on myself. I told them about the others, not really knowing anything about it, and gave them the lame reasons for why I did it. Thinking my truthfulness would let me go home, they told me to stand up, put me in handcuffs, and off to jail I went.

CHAPTER SIX

Made The News

If you've ever been locked up, you know the thoughts of what you should have done and what you shouldn't have done begin to consume your mind. I called my wife to find out they had also busted the doors down at my place and gone through the house. Thank Jesus, there was nothing there for them to use against me. She asked if I was going to tell my parents. I said, "Heck naw." I mean, how disappointed were they going to be when they found this out? There was no way I was going to do that. I figured I'd let it quietly go without them even knowing anything.

Just as I finished that thought, she said, "You're gonna have to. It's on the news."

I looked up, and there it was on the morning news—with a big, nice picture of my face. I remember feeling so embarrassed that it made me cry. I put my shirt over my face, and it all just came out. After I let that out, I finally called my parents. I was still crying a little bit.

If you know my mom, you know she was very encouraging and told me it was going to be okay. All the stuff that helped fuel my tears because I could sense in her voice that she was worried too. I finally talked to my father. He's different. He's going to talk strong faith no matter what. Expecting to hear something profound from him, he got on the phone and said, "You better get in the Word of God and find out what God wants to do with your life."

WHAT?! That's the advice he was giving me right now? I was hoping he knew a lawyer or something. I wasn't in the position to hear what God's plan was now—I wanted God to get me out of jail. That was not what I wanted to hear, but it sure was what I needed to hear.

About 12 hours later, I was released and finally home. Trying to figure out the next move, I found a lawyer who laid out the federal charges against me and the time I was facing. I remember him telling me that, with the current charges, I would be facing the possibility of 20-plus years.

I was like, *What the heck did they think I did? 20 years? What is that?* But heck, the numbers were in the millions for the merchandise I had "allegedly" taken. On the night I got caught, I had close to $200,000 worth of stuff alone. Thinking about how long I had been doing it, that number must have added up to 20 years.

It was in this moment that I remembered those words my father had said to me. I needed to get in the Word and find out what God wanted to do with my life, because surely He didn't want me to go to prison for 20 years. If His plan included me doing any time in prison, that was not the plan I wanted to follow. I knew I needed a miracle, and I knew I was in a position to believe God for it because of the ministry I had always heard my father preach about.

I Need a Miracle

One of my father's first books was called *You Can Be Set Free*, and it detailed his life of crime and how God had worked a miracle in his life when he was supposed to get 60 years in prison but only did 10 months. That was the same miracle I needed, so it only made sense to do it the same way my father did. I mean, with all the evidence against me, my only hope was going to be God. The lawyer was not feeling the thought of me not doing any time, so my mention of that often came with laughter on his part.

Nevertheless, I went about believing God for my miracle the only way I knew how. By faith, by speaking the Word of God and nothing else. It seemed like the easiest thing to do, but time would show that this process is only for the strong at heart.

I was arrested in October of that year (2010), and though now needing a miracle, I was into God again, I still had some unfinished business with the outside world that I needed to take care of. One of those things was a trip to

Miami that we had planned before all the chaos. You know, I wasn't going to let this whole case interrupt my chance to kick it in Miami for the first time. So, I went on that trip.

When we first got there, I received a call from my lawyer telling me the first offer from the courts. I remember we were sitting down having lunch, and I went outside to take the call. I can still see the tan building of the restaurant we were eating at and remember seeing a nice Ferrari driving down the street. I was looking at my friends eating and laughing when I heard the lawyer say the words, "They are talking about 20 years."

That broke my whole heart, and at that moment, I knew my life was over. There was no way God was going to get me out of this. I broke down crying and began to reflect on my life at that point. It felt like it had all been a waste if I was going to be locked up for that long. I pulled myself together and decided that if this was going to be it, I might as well live it up. I still had a belief that God would work it out, but in the back of my mind (now I know it was the devil), I just knew I was going to do some time in prison. This mountain seemed too insurmountable for me at that time.

I had a good time in Miami. I often tell the story about the time I went to a club in Miami, and LeBron James was there (it was when he first went to Miami), so the club was off the chain. At one point, we were in VIP right across from him and his team. I wanted to flex a little, so me and my guys always had this thing about throwing money down to the crowd. We started throwing ones, and the whole crowd turned around and started vibing in front of us. Next thing I know, someone from that area started throwing ones back. That did not sit well with me, so we started throwing fives. Then they came back with twenties, and we were done.

When I came back home a couple of weeks later after that vacation, I had a birthday party planned. Again, I wasn't going to let this case take my joy, so I went to my party and lived it up once again. With everything that was going on and my tendency to party, I felt myself slipping back into that old way of living. You know, believing in God when it was crazy, but living any way I wanted to.

A few days after the party, my father called me. Thinking this was just a check-up call, he mentioned the party. Someone had told him about the birthday bash (I think it was my little sister). He gave me some of the best advice that I live by even today. He said, "You can't expect a miracle from God and live any kind of way."

I recall those words hitting me deep on the inside. I knew that for what I needed from God, I had to do something different from what I had always done. After all, the desire for this lifestyle was what had landed me in this situation in the first place. I had always played the role of a Christian, but still had things in my life that didn't seem to edify God. I knew that for this, I needed to be totally sold out. I didn't want to get a miracle just to end up back in the same situation again, and that would have happened if I continued living the way I was at the time.

The Journey Begins

After this, I started the process of refocusing on getting my miracle from God. I stopped hanging out and **immersed** myself in reading and studying the Word, specifically for my miracle. I still had some money left over from that lifestyle, so for a while, the walk of faith was easy for me. That lasted up until the money ran out because at that time, my wife was paying all the bills, and I could not get a job because of the case.

It slowly began to get tougher, and I found myself in multiple fights, needing multiple victories from God. On one hand, I was focusing on fighting this case, which was the most important thing in my eyes. Then there were the bills that started to **weigh** on my wife. As you can imagine, with all of that going on, it caused stress in the marriage, and it did a pretty good job on us. It got to a point where I was sleeping on the couch and hardly speaking with her.

This was a rough time for me. In dealing with thoughts of going to prison and losing my family and freedom, I found myself in a place where it seemed like I was alone in this. With no one to talk to, I developed a deeper relationship with God. Those nights sleeping on the couch turned into nights of begging and praying to God to fix my life and make things better. If you have ever been seeking God while at your lowest, you know what that process entails, and you know the attacks that the enemy plays with your mind during those times.

With no one to talk to and nowhere to run, I began to develop a numbness toward people. I knew God was there, but I began to lose hope in people. I felt like everyone around me was expecting me to go to prison (besides my parents, of course). By this time, I had spent so much time in the Word and away from people that I became a Jesus freak, and every word I spoke was in relation to Him.

I remember the lawyer would call me in and tell me the new deal, and I would say, "I'm not taking any deal because I am not going to prison." I would come home from court or from seeing the lawyer, and my wife would ask me how it went. Even though they had just offered me 16 years, I would say, "It's looking good. I am not going to do one day in prison."

While I knew the situation was saying otherwise, I had fully understood the power of positive confession. So I only spoke about the things that I wanted to happen in my life. I remember one of my prayers at that time was that I was never going to have handcuffs put on me ever again. I would pray this every night and stand on the promises of God for this not to happen.

It had been a year since everything had happened, and I had not heard anything from my lawyer in months. It had been so long since I had heard anything that I thought God had worked the miracle and they had just forgotten about me.

Man, was I wrong.

Back In Handcuffs

One night, while finishing up my nightly routine of praying and seeking God, around two or three in the morning, there was a ring at the door. Not thinking anything too big about it, I opened the door in my shorts and socks to the Carmel Police Department with a search warrant for my arrest. I was so heartbroken.

The devil immediately said to me, "This is it. You're going to spend 20 years in prison." "Your wife is going to leave you." "It's over now."

I remember thinking, *How could God let this happen when I constantly pray that I touch no more handcuffs?* My faith was definitely rattled, and I was no longer sure that God was on my side, or even heard me, for that matter.

There I was, sitting in the Hamilton County Jail, wondering how God was going to work this out. I sat in the holding area most of that day. I was grateful that I was in Hamilton County Jail as opposed to Marion County Jail (if you know, you know). They finally put me in one of the blocks. It was peaceful and calm in there, and on my bunk was an old-school Gideon Bible. I picked it up and began where I left off—Psalm 91. I read that verse over and over, day after day. I did not eat, I did not drink, just stayed in that Word. It was the only thing keeping me from losing my mind based on all the lies the enemy was saying in my head.

I was transported to Marion County Jail a week later and was sent back to the processing center. I did not know what was going on at that point. I just knew I did not want to go across the street to the jail. I was finally bonded out and was able to get back home. I remember this most because I had to sell one of the cars that I really liked to pay back the money.

Still not knowing what was happening, I went to see my lawyer, and he told me that it was a good thing that I got locked up. Wondering how on earth that could be a good thing, he then told me that the feds dropped the case and the state picked it up. I was thinking, *God, you did not have to send me to jail for that.*

He said the state would be more lenient and that we could work with them better than the feds. He then said they still had the same charges on me and were offering close to 15 years. By this time, I was still confident in my confession and told him the same thing I had been saying: I am not going to prison. I recall him getting irritated and saying something to the effect of, "Now William, we are not going to start with this again." What he did not realize was that I was fully invested in believing God was going to work a miracle. So I was not changing my confession. It had kept me out of jail to that point, and I was too far in to go back.

After a while, the conversations turned to taking a plea deal or starting to get ready for trial. After one of those meetings, I was driving home when the Holy Spirit said to me, "Take it to trial." That thought was a rough one because I knew they caught me with the stuff, had witnesses against me, and I confessed to it. Taking it to trial would have most assuredly led to a conviction, but I was trusting in God, so I was going to do it His way.

So over the course of the next year, I went back and forth, turning down deals under the premise that I was not going to do one day in prison. Finally, one day, my lawyer called me in and said, "William, we have a good deal on the table. They are offering you two years, and with good behavior and this being your first offense, you could be out in 10 months." He then said, "This is the last offer they are willing to give you."

I remember immediately saying, "Good, because this is the last time I have to tell you that I am not going to prison."

He let out a deep breath and offered me my money back, but of course, he was just joking. He said okay and went back to tell them what I said.

Added Stress

Now, as you can imagine, by this time, money was getting tight in the house. I had not been able to get a job due to my pending case, and my wife was paying all the bills as the money we had saved was pretty much gone. I was not as concerned about a job and bills as I was about staying out of prison, but this also added to the stress of potentially going to prison and leaving my family.

One day, as I was in prayer about all of this, the Word of the Lord came to me and said that if I was living by faith, then I had to live like I was already free and get on with my life. That day, I adopted a new attitude that I was going to live as if the situation had already been taken care of. I was going to act like I was free and begin looking for jobs. I also enrolled in my MBA during this time.

From this experience with God that day, I coined the phrase "Live Free, Trust God," and I have lived by this saying every day since. I would get up in the morning, take a shower, get dressed, and act like I was going to work. We had a mirror in our bathroom that went the whole length of the wall, and I would walk back and forth with my Bible in my hand, preaching the Word to myself in that mirror for hours while I was at home alone. My faith at this time was so focused on God that I just knew in my heart He would deliver me.

After a few months, I was working for a temp agency, and I just knew that I was not supposed to be there. But times were rough, and I needed to bring some money into the house. That lasted for about a month. Then one day, I just walked off the job.

Still looking for a job, one of the guys from my parents' Jesus House was working for a specific non-profit organization. They were looking for someone to work the front desk overnight, and since most nights I was up all night anyway, I decided to take the job. It was part-time and only paid $8.25 an hour, but I was sleeping on the couch at the time, so anything was better than nothing.

Once I finally got the job, my lawyer called me and told me that I was due to be in court the next week to start the process for going to trial. This brought about another test of my faith.

Two Part Process

Over the years, the one thing I have learned when standing in faith is that there are two parts to the process. The first is your confession and believing that God is going to work a miracle. In this process, faith is easy because you are simply building yourself up for the day of truth. Then there is the second process: the day of truth, the day when you find out if your faith all this time was legit or just a way to get you through. This is the day when all the fear and doubt hit you at once. This is where the devil is telling you nonstop that you did not do enough and that everything you have been believing for is about to come crashing down. This is the part of the process where fear becomes its most powerful. Just the thought that I could be going to court, and any day I could walk in and not come back out for a while. This part was hard, and it was upon me, and I had nothing left but to stand on faith in God's Word.

There were no more deals, there were no more options—this was it. Was God going to get me through, or had I just spent the last two years of my life dreaming and wishing for some magic? One thing I do remember thinking was that if Jesus let me go to prison, I was going to be done with Him and all the fake faith stuff that my father had told me about for all these years. Now before you look at me funny for that, please understand that I was totally trusting in God through this whole process. I had turned down deal after deal on the premise that I believed that God would deliver me. Had I not gotten delivered, I would have been so disappointed in my trust over the last couple of years. I was not ready to face that. I was not ready to think about God in the light of Him not being able to work it out. I was not ready to see God fail—not at this moment, not when He had meant so much to me at this time.

If you recall earlier, I said that my lawyer told me that there would be no more deals made after that last conversation, so my father and I went to court that day, not knowing what to expect. We arrived at court, and as we sat there, I heard my father next to me praying in tongues. I myself was thinking in tongues. You know how you get in situations and don't want to say anything or pray? That's how I was. I did not know what to say or pray, so I was just thinking in tongues, too nervous to open my mouth.

As we sat there, the lawyer walked into the courtroom and did not even acknowledge me. He just went straight to the prosecutor and started talking. As I nervously watched, I saw him shake her hand, then look at me and gesture for me and my father to go wait outside. At this point, my nerves were at their highest because it looked like we were not going to go in front of the judge that day, but I did not know exactly what that meant.

While in the lobby, my father went over to the corner to continue to pray in the Spirit. I heard him over there, and he was really going at it. After about 10–15 minutes, my lawyer finally came out. As he walked up, he said, "Not sure what God is doing, but…" Before he could finish, I heard my father suddenly stop praying. Then he finished with, "But they have offered you another deal." I could sense my father with a smile on his face.

I was thinking, *What deal could be better than the last one unless it did not include prison time?*

He then told me that the state was offering to drop all of the felonies except for one, and with that, they would give me six months of house arrest and six months of probation—no prison time. Then he asked, "Do you want that deal?"

I often say I almost went to jail that day because I almost slapped him when he asked me that. Of course, I wanted that deal.

On that day, I walked out of court the happiest man in Indiana. That is the day I knew that my God could literally do anything. I could not wait to get to my phone to tell my wife and others the news of how standing on God's Word had come through for me in the clutch. I was so overjoyed that I could hardly believe it was true. No more worrying late nights about my life. No more wondering if I needed to go on the run or commit suicide. No more worrying about my freedom. Two years' worth of stress just gone in an instant because of the goodness of God.

A few weeks later, we went to court to deal with the plea agreement and sentencing, and I was immediately put on my house arrest band. I walked out of there proud of my little band, not worrying about what others would think. Heck, they had no idea what I had to go through to get that band, and I was not going to be ashamed of it. After all, I had gotten myself into that situation, and for me, it was a testament to what God can do in anyone's life if they just choose to believe in Him.

It was at this moment, those many years ago, that I decided to live for Jesus no matter what comes. I immediately applied those two years of principles that I had learned to every other area of my life. I was determined to live free and trust in my God.

CHAPTER SEVEN

With that situation behind me, it was time for me to get back to my life and figure out what the next plan was. I was working at that same non-profit place, but that was because no one else would hire me. I figured I would just stay there for now since I was in school and on house arrest. It was a good place for me to work on the 3rd shift. I was still in the doghouse at home, and the 3rd shift allowed me to sleep in the bed during the day and not on the couch.

I stayed faithful to God on that job, as it was definitely a humbling experience for me. Here I was, college-educated, and was being led by people who weren't. Not to mention, I would take that little check home to my wife, and it seemed as though she was looking at me with this look of disgust. If you have ever experienced that look, you know how it makes you feel on the inside. She would give me the check back and say stuff like, "I can't do anything with that."

All of this initially was a tough pill to swallow, but I had this new understanding of God and how He can do anything if I just continued to trust in Him. So I learned to deal with it. I stayed faithful to the job. I did not sleep. I made sure it was always clean. I worked as unto the Lord. I worked that job with grace and even had the chance to continue to share Jesus with those that I came across.

After about 6 months, I was off the band and was ready to do something different. While seeking God, another part-time position within the company came up, and I was asked to take the position. It was still part-time and only paid $11.25 an hour, but it was a step up and more of a professional feel that suited my liking. It still got me the looks of disgust on payday, but again, I stayed faithful to God, reading and studying the Word, and completing my MBA.

About 2 months after that, I was promoted again to full-time with full benefits. I often say that when you take full-time benefits home, you no longer have to sleep on the couch. This time, when the checks came home, my wife now had a smile on her face. I knew that smile meant that she was taking some of this check, and I was okay with it because I no longer saw that same look of disgust.

Things were going well in my life with Christ, and after a year, I was ready to move on again. I had just finished my MBA, and there was an opening for the assistant director job within my organization. I met all the requirements and had been receiving accolades for the work I was doing. So I decided to put my name in the hat.

I had heard that they had other people in line, but I figured I might as well at least let them know what my credentials were. I applied, and after about a month, I started to hear how they had gotten it all figured out and had people in place. I was so upset that they had done all of this and did not even give me a chance to interview.

Frustrated, I decided I was going to leave that organization and see what my MBA would do for me elsewhere. I remember that weekend I stayed online looking for other opportunities and filling out applications, just trusting in God to lead me the right way.

On Monday, I got to work and received a call from my Director telling me that he wanted to meet with me. I had figured that he had heard I was looking elsewhere and wanted to scold me for being so outspoken about it. He sat me down and asked me what my inspirations were and how I would go about making things better in another position. Of course, I told him, and in the back of my mind, I was thinking why he would be asking me that.

Once I finished, he told me how impressed he had been with my work over the last year and that he felt that I had the ability to lead in another area. He then told me that the plan that I had been hearing about included me, and the assistant director position I had applied for was mine.

Overjoyed with what God was doing in my life at this time, I began to dig deeper into His Word, searching and wanting more. Then, about a year and a half after that, I was promoted again to the director of the facility with about 25 staff members under me. God had been so faithful to me at this point.

Within 3 years from the time I had made that mistake, God had completely restored my life. My marriage was doing great, and a few years later, we had our second daughter, the same year we moved into our new house. After about 6 years of working as the director, I went back to school to pursue my doctorate degree at Liberty University, and in 2023, I received that degree. My dissertation was about the effects that faith can have on prisoners and how Christ can restore lives if you trust in Him. My instructor told me that it was one of the best dissertations he had ever read.

I faithfully worked as the director of that facility for 10 years. I was blessed to share the gospel with so many and see many of those same lives change from following the same steps I did by simply trusting in the Word of God. In 2024, I left there and went into ministry with my parents, and now I spend my time doing the one thing that I ran from for so long—prison ministry. I knew that this was what God was calling me to do from the beginning. I knew in college, I knew when I came home from college, I knew when I worked for that company, and I knew when I worked as the director. For so long, I ran away from that call, and it caused some real chaos in my life.

Now that I am in the will of God, there is no more chaos. Sure, things get rough, and troubles and setbacks come, but I do not have to worry about them because I found out when I was facing all of that time in prison that God can even work out the chaos. I mentioned earlier how my father wrote a book called *You Can Be Set Free*, which chronicles his testimony of how God delivered him from a life of crime and supernaturally set him free from a potential 60-year sentence. He outlined a plan for success in that book for a miracle, and I found myself needing the same miracle he needed.

All I did was follow the plan from the book. I gave my life to Christ, started to read His Word, then I believed His Word, and finally I trusted in and acted on His Word. When I did those things, God worked a miracle in my life. I now realize that all I had to do in the beginning was to put my heart into Him in the same way, and I would not have gone through all of that.

This is the reason I wrote this book. You may be going through a tough situation in your life. You may be in prison needing a time cut. You may be on trial needing a miracle. You may just need a job or simply want peace and freedom in your life. Like me, you may have tried everything else in the world trying to get that freedom, and it just never comes. I urge you to give your life to Jesus and let Him guide you to that freedom like He did for me. His Word invites us to come to Him if we are weary and heavy-laden, and He promises to give us rest (Matthew 11:28).

Whatever it is that you need freedom from, Jesus wants to give it to you. Please do not hesitate any longer to give your life to Him today.

If you do just like me, YOU CAN BE SET FREE TOO!

www.ingramcontent.com/pod-product-compliance
Lightning Source LLC
Chambersburg PA
CBHW061330050726
47595CB00005B/1854

9781971694511